Original title:
The Silent Chill

Copyright © 2024 Swan Charm
All rights reserved.

Author: Paula Raudsepp
ISBN HARDBACK: 978-9916-79-453-1
ISBN PAPERBACK: 978-9916-79-454-8
ISBN EBOOK: 978-9916-79-455-5

Secrets in the Frozen Air

Whispers float on icy breath,
Tales of winter's quiet death.
Starlit nights, the world so still,
Nature's secrets, hearts to fill.

Frosty patterns dress the trees,
Dancing gently in the breeze.
Underneath the silence lies,
Echoes of the past arise.

Winter's Veil of Silence

Veils of white conceal the earth,
Blankets soft, a time of mirth.
Snowflakes flutter, lost in grace,
Each one tells a tale in space.

Moonlight casts a silver glow,
Shadows shift on powdered snow.
In the hush, the world breathes slow,
Winter's whispers, soft and low.

Creep of the Arctic Breeze

Chill winds weave through frozen trees,
A gentle touch from distant seas.
Secrets ride on each cool sigh,
Stories of the winter sky.

Crystals sparkle, nature's art,
Carving beauty, winter's heart.
As night falls, the shadows blend,
In the cool, all time suspends.

Hushed Crystals on the Ground

Softly resting all around,
Nature's gems on frosty ground.
Every glimmer, every spark,
Holds a story in the dark.

Footsteps muffled, silence calls,
In winter's realm, the stillness falls.
Beneath the stars, a world transforms,
In the quiet, beauty soars.

A Blanket of Whispered Winter

The snowflakes dance, soft and light,
Gently falling, purest white.
Whispers echo through the trees,
A world wrapped up in winter's freeze.

Quiet nights, the stars aglow,
Winter's breath, a chilling flow.
Footsteps hushed on frozen ground,
Nature's beauty all around.

Frosted windows, a secret view,
Warmth inside, a fire's hue.
Each flake unique, a story spun,
Under the gaze of a frosty sun.

In the stillness, time does pause,
Reflecting on the silent cause.
The world transformed, a wintry spell,
In this blanket, we dwell well.

As dawn breaks with a tender glow,
Softly melting the winter's show.
Memories linger, sweet and bright,
In a blanket of whispered night.

Frosted Secrets Kept Untold

Underneath the moon's soft glare,
Secrets drift upon the air.
Frosted leaves, a tale concealed,
Whispers in the night revealed.

Icicles hang like dreams enshrined,
Frozen thoughts, a heart entwined.
In the silence, stories grow,
Frosted secrets, quiet and slow.

Beneath the snow, a world unknown,
Silent paths where shadows moan.
Each step taken in midnight's glow,
Unravels secrets buried low.

Winter's chill, a spell so deep,
Echoes of the trees that weep.
Hidden truths in icy seams,
Frosted moments turn to dreams.

As sunlight breaks the frozen night,
Revealing all in gentle light.
Still, some secrets choose to stay,
Frosted whispers fade away.

Frozen Leaves in Twilight

Leaves hang still, caught in dusk's light,
Whispers of frost in the fading sight.
Colors subdued, nature's sigh,
Frozen memories as moments fly.

Twilight dances on brittle ground,
Echoes of summer, softly found.
A world transformed into a dream,
Where silence mingles with the gleam.

Glistening veins through muted hues,
Nature's canvas, shaped by the blues.
In stillness deep, a story weaves,
Of frozen leaves in twilight eves.

Shadows on the Frosted Ground

Footsteps whisper on the ice,
Shadows weaving, soft and nice.
Frosty breath in the early morn,
Nature's palette, quietly worn.

Branches bare against the dawn,
Painting shadows, crisp and drawn.
The world asleep, in silence shrouded,
Where once the warmth, now cold is clouded.

Each print a tale of where we roam,
Echoes left far from home.
Underneath the winter's spell,
Shadows linger, weave and swell.

Lullabies of the Icy Night

Moonlight bathes the sleeping earth,
In icy whispers, a gentle birth.
Stars twinkle softly, a silver song,
Lullabies drift, where dreams belong.

Beneath the frost, the world breathes slow,
Wrapped in warmth of a winter glow.
Melodies rise with the chilly air,
Serenades weave through night so rare.

Winds hum softly, caressing trees,
Carrying tales of winter's ease.
In the dark, hope takes its flight,
Lullabies of the icy night.

Choreography of Snowflakes

Falling softly from skies so clear,
Snowflakes dance, a ballet near.
Spinning gently to the ground,
Whirls of white without a sound.

Each unique, a wonder spun,
A fleeting moment, a sparkling run.
Frozen twirls in the winter air,
Nature's art, a dream laid bare.

As they gather, a quilt is made,
Underfoot, a soft cascade.
In their journey, beauty thrives,
Choreography of snowflake lives.

Veiled Shapes in Snowfall

Silent shadows drift and dance,
Whispers wrapped in white expanse.
Footprints linger, faint yet bright,
Mysterious forms in the pale light.

Branches bow with weighty grace,
Nature's quilt, a soft embrace.
Time stands still, as snowflakes weave,
Veiled secrets that we believe.

Glistening roofs, a wonderland,
Frosted lace, by winter's hand.
Echoed laughter, muffled, low,
In this hush, we find the glow.

Every flake tells a tale of old,
In this stillness, dreams unfold.
Underneath the silent night,
Veiled shapes swirl in soft twilight.

Breath of the Frigid Earth

Frozen whispers fill the air,
Life holds its breath in silent prayer.
Nature sleeps beneath the chill,
Veins of frost, a timeless thrill.

Branches wear their crystal crowns,
Silent stories scatter down.
In the stillness, secrets lie,
Beneath the vast, unending sky.

The earth exhales, a frosty sigh,
In every corner, spirits fly.
Roots entwined with icy breath,
Life defies the coldest death.

Beneath the snow, the world awaits,
Dreaming softly of warmer fates.
Time will thaw the frozen ground,
When spring returns, life will abound.

When Silence Falls Like Snow

When silence falls, the world takes pause,
Wrapped in stillness, without cause.
The evening air, so crisp and clear,
Whispers echo, drawing near.

Patterns form as flakes descend,
Softly blanketing, a gentle friend.
Blank walls listen, secrets shared,
In this silence, hearts are bared.

Branches sigh beneath the weight,
Each soft flake, a fateful fate.
The world slows down, a sacred glow,
In the hush, our spirits flow.

Time is lost in a dreamlike state,
Each breath held, we contemplate.
When silence falls like snow tonight,
We find our peace, our soft twilight.

Distant Murmurs in the Frost

In the chill, a quiet sound,
Distant murmurs wrap around.
Frosty air, a timeless sigh,
Echoes linger, never die.

Footsteps crunch on frozen ground,
Silence weaves a gentle bound.
Whispers of the past remain,
Carried softly, like the rain.

Branches sway, as if to talk,
In this quiet, shadows walk.
Every flake a tale retold,
In their dance, the night's unfold.

Crisp and clear, the night unveils,
Secrets hidden in the gales.
Distant murmurs fill the night,
In the frost, we find our light.

Gray Horizons in the Frost

Gray skies loom over fields,
Silent whispers in the breeze.
Each breath is cold, yet calm,
Nature sleeps beneath the freeze.

Footprints trace a path of dreams,
Memories linger in the air.
Whispers call from distant lands,
Echoes of a time more fair.

Trees stand dressed in icy coats,
Branches draped like fragile lace.
The world feels soft, a muted hush,
Wrapped in winter's cold embrace.

Time slows down as shadows stretch,
While the sun begins to fade.
Colors dim in the heart of frost,
Nature's light begins to shade.

In this quiet, gray exhale,
Hope pauses, yet it's still here.
Underneath the frozen still,
Life awaits the springtime cheer.

A Canvas of Melancholy and Snow

A canvas paints itself in white,
Blank spaces hold the weight of thought.
Every flake, a memory lost,
Innocent dreams that time forgot.

Footsteps on the pitted ground,
Echoes fade in winter's breath.
Where laughter danced in summers past,
Now silence shrouds the warmth of flesh.

Branches bow with heavy crowns,
The sky weeps frosty tears.
Nature wears a cloak of sorrow,
A silent witness to our fears.

In the stillness, shadows play,
Figures lost in drifting snow.
We find solace in the chill,
Amidst the beauty, hearts still grow.

This canvas holds both joy and pain,
In hues that only winter brings.
Underneath the frozen surface,
Lie stories waiting on frozen wings.

Whispers of Frost

Whispers of frost in the air,
Secrets told by the chilly breeze.
With every breath, a tale unfolds,
Snowflakes dancing among the trees.

The world is wrapped in silken white,
Soft as dreams that drift away.
Underneath each layer of ice,
Silent hopes and wishes stay.

Morning light plays tricks on time,
Sparkling jewels in the dawn.
Frosted voices softly mingle,
In this hush, a new day is born.

Nature holds her breath in awe,
Wonders woven in winter's thread.
Each flake, a promise of tomorrow,
In the stillness, life quietly spread.

Beneath the frost, there lies a pulse,
A rhythm waiting, deep below.
Listen closely, hear the whispers,
In the silence, love will grow.

Echoes Beneath the Ice

Echoes beneath the surface wait,
Memories frozen in time's embrace.
Each ripple hides a story told,
In crystalline silence, they trace.

Underneath the frozen sheets,
Life sleeps deep, close to the core.
Whispers of warmth from days gone by,
Echo softly, forevermore.

The world above may seem so still,
Yet beneath, there's a pulse alive.
In the depths of winter's womb,
Hidden joys and dreams will thrive.

When the sun begins to shine,
And thaw reveals what's been concealed,
A symphony of colors burst,
Life returns, its fate revealed.

So let us cherish these cold days,
For in the frost, we find our way.
Echoes teach us to stand tall,
In the quiet, hope finds its say.

A Breath of Icy Serenity

In winter's hush, the world lies still,
A silver veil, a silent chill.
Snowflakes dance on whispered breeze,
Nature's peace, a tranquil freeze.

Branches bow with frosted weight,
Each breath sharp, a moment's fate.
The moonlight glimmers on ice-bound streams,
Unraveling softly, fragile dreams.

Through the stillness, shadows creep,
As night surrounds, secrets keep.
A breath of icy serenity flows,
In this quiet, the heart knows.

Frost adorns the barren trees,
Fingers trace the cold, white leaves.
Each crystal sparkles, a fleeting time,
Whispers linger in rhythm and rhyme.

So breathe in deep, let worries fade,
In winter's realm, calmness is laid.
Nature's canvas, pure and bright,
A breath of peace, a tender light.

Frostbitten Reflections

Mirror lakes, a somber glow,
Captured dreams lie soft below.
Every ripple tells a tale,
Of winter's breath, a frosted veil.

Shadows flicker, moments freeze,
In the stillness, hearts appease.
Frostbitten whispers in the air,
Echoes linger, distant flare.

Silent woods adorned in white,
A haunting beauty, pure delight.
Time stands still, as dusk descends,
Where nature's grace and sorrow blend.

Ghostly figures, past entwined,
Reflections fade in this bind.
Each step careful, on the edge,
Of memories, a frozen pledge.

In the twilight, secrets gleam,
A tapestry of dusk's sweet dream.
Frostbitten visions, soft and clear,
In this silence, we persevere.

Muffled Secrets of the Dark

In shadows deep, the secrets hide,
Muffled echoes, softly bide.
A world covered in night's embrace,
Where dreams and fears find space.

Whispers linger in chilling air,
Each breath held, a silent prayer.
Beneath the stars, stories wait,
In hushed tones, we contemplating fate.

Pale moonlight drapes the earth in grace,
Illuminating every face.
Muffled secrets, softly told,
In the heart, they gleam like gold.

Night's tender arms, a fierce embrace,
Sheltering hopes, in darkness trace.
Every shadow, a chilling thought,
Lessons learned and battles fought.

So listen close, to silence deep,
In the dark, the secrets seep.
Muffled whispers, guidance near,
A reminder, we hold dear.

Silence Beneath the Snow

In the quiet, snowflakes fall,
Covering earth, a soft call.
Each layer deepens, secrets flow,
A world transformed, in purest glow.

Fields once vibrant, now sleep tight,
Wrapped in white, a tranquil sight.
Beneath the surface, life remains,
In whispered dreams, love sustains.

Footprints mark the frosty trail,
Echoes of laughter, tales unveil.
Silence reigns, a gentle shield,
In this stillness, hearts are healed.

The world slows down, each breath clear,
With every flake, we shed our fear.
Silence washes over the land,
In winter's arms, we understand.

So let the snow wrap us tight,
In its comfort, find the light.
Silence beneath, both vast and rare,
A moment's peace, beyond compare.

Softly Whispered Goodbyes

In the twilight dim, we part,
Words hang heavy like the night.
Promises linger in the air,
While shadows stretch towards the light.

Tears glisten like morning dew,
On petals, soft, and tender wide.
Each sigh a gentle farewell tune,
Carried on the waves of pride.

Memories dance like fireflies,
In the corners of our mind.
Every glance a fleeting kiss,
Eternally intertwined.

The clock ticks with quiet grace,
Time moves on, yet here we stay.
In the heart, our stories weave,
Softly whispered, fade away.

Echoes of the Crystal Embrace

In the dawn of winter's breath,
Silence wraps the world like lace.
Crystal branches, gently sway,
Whispering of love's embrace.

Footsteps crunch on frosty ground,
Each echo holds a secret tight.
Nature weaves a tale profound,
In shadows danced by silver light.

The air is crisp, it bites and curls,
Yet warmth blooms in the heart's core.
As laughter flutters through the cold,
And dreams awaken to explore.

Beneath the frost, life lies in wait,
Spring's promise softly lingers.
In the stillness, hope ignites,
With every line the cold life fingers.

Heartbeats Under Winter's Cloak

Beneath the stars, we lay entwined,
The world is wrapped in slumber deep.
Breathless whispers, hearts aligned,
In the night, our secrets keep.

With every beat, the silence grows,
A rhythm matched by nature's song.
Chilled air stirs, love's warmth flows,
In this moment, we belong.

Snowflakes dance like fleeting dreams,
Each one unique, a gentle thread.
Underneath the moon's soft beams,
We find our magic, love widespread.

The universe is ours to hold,
In the echoes of the night air.
Wrapped in winter's purest gold,
Our hearts beat strong, beyond compare.

The Hush of Falling Snow

As night descends, the world turns white,
Silence blankets every street.
In the hush, there lies delight,
Each flake a kiss, soft and sweet.

Windows glow, a beacon bright,
While shadows play with quiet grace.
In this moment, still and light,
Time slows down, we find our place.

Cocoa warms our frozen hands,
Laughter echoes in the night.
As winter weaves its gentle strands,
Every corner feels just right.

And outside, snowflakes dance and swirl,
Like memories caught in a dream.
With every twirl, the heart's unfurled,
In this embrace, we softly gleam.

Murmurs of the Icy Twilight

In the stillness of the dusk,
Whispers waltz through frozen air,
Stars twinkle with a gentle glow,
A secret shared, a silent prayer.

Cold embraces every sound,
Nature breathes a breath of peace,
Softly echoing all around,
In this moment, troubles cease.

Moonlight drapes the world in white,
Casting shadows on the ground,
Crystal flakes begin to dance,
As silence holds the night profound.

Frosty hands reach for the sky,
Dreams of warmth, just out of sight,
Yet there lies a serene trust,
In the murmurs of the twilight light.

Each breath taken, sharp and bright,
A fleeting warmth through chilly night.

Shadows Cast by Quiet Frost

Beneath the tree where shadows fall,
Frost whispers tales of days gone past,
A hush ensues, a gentle call,
Nature holds its breath, steadfast.

Moonlit paths are paved in white,
Echoing the still of night,
Thoughts like snowflakes softly drift,
Caught in dreams, elusive gift.

Hushed reflections find their place,
In the glimmer of the frost,
Memories of a fleeting race,
Nothing gained and nothing lost.

The world adorned in crystalline,
Every branch a muse, a rhyme,
The quiet lingers, pure and fine,
Eternal beauty, frozen time.

In the breath of winter's air,
Shadows dance without a care.

Lament of the Withered Leaves

Once vibrant hues now faded brown,
Leaves whisper softly to the ground,
Their rustle tells of time's cruel sway,
In every sigh, a parting sound.

Once they danced in summer's sun,
Now they lay in silence deep,
Each a story left unspun,
In loneliness, they barely weep.

Through the chill, their spirits roam,
Haunted by what once was bright,
Yet in this shade, they find a home,
Adapting to the coming night.

A tapestry of gold and rust,
Nature's art, so bittersweet,
Through the wind, they learn to trust,
In the ebb of life's retreat.

Lament sweetly, withered friends,
Each season's change, a cycle bends.

The Breath of the Winter Night

Underneath the velvet sky,
Winter breathes a tale untold,
Chill of night begins to sigh,
In its grasp, the world turns cold.

Stars appear like scattered dreams,
Glittering in a frosty haze,
Among the pines, a silence beams,
Wrapped in moonlight's silver gaze.

With each breath, the stillness grows,
Nature rests, a peaceful rest,
Beneath the drape of winter's prose,
A tender heart within its chest.

In the shadows, secrets creep,
The dance of night softly churns,
Memories held in dreams we keep,
As the world, in slumber, turns.

And with the dawn, a light awakes,
But for now, the winter takes.

Hushed Hearts in Winter

In the quiet of the night,
Snowflakes drift and swirl,
Hearts embrace the stillness,
Winter's quiet pearl.

Whispers dance on frosty air,
Soft sighs of snow below,
In the grasp of icy hands,
Time begins to slow.

Branches bare beneath the weight,
Cloaked in glistening white,
Nature's breath holds secrets,
In the hush of night.

Stars peek through the cloudy veil,
A blanket smooth and deep,
Lost in thoughts of warmth and life,
As the world lies asleep.

Every heartbeat echoes clear,
In the frosted embrace,
Calling softly to the dawn,
Waiting for its grace.

Veil of Breathless Cold

Underneath a silver sky,
The world lies wrapped in white,
Frosted windows tell a tale,
Of whispers in the night.

Each breath forms a fragile cloud,
Invisible and bright,
A silent promise lingers,
In the veil of breathless night.

Footsteps crunch on frozen ground,
Echoes in the freeze,
Nature holds its fragile breath,
In the stillness, peace.

Winds that swirl and twist around,
Singing through the trees,
Eagles soar on icy drafts,
In searches for their ease.

The night creeps closer, shadows dance,
Wrapped in moonlit glow,
Embracing the heart's stillness,
In a world dressed in snow.

Shadows in the Frosted Air

A silhouette of folded limbs,
Beneath the winter's breath,
Shadows cast on icy ground,
    Whisper tales of death.

Life retreats to hidden realms,
Cocooned in chilling night,
Every glimmer, every gleam,
In shadows, takes to flight.

Silent trees adorn their crowns,
With frost as their delight,
Each branch points to the heavens,
In a dance of muted light.

The air is thick with stories,
Of warmth and things once near,
In every breath of frosted air,
    Echoes reappear.

And so we sit in quiet peace,
Among the shadows cast,
Holding close the fleeting warmth,
As winter's spell holds fast.

Lullaby of Frozen Dreams

In the night's embrace we find,
A lullaby of snow,
With every flake that tumbles down,
A whispered tale of woe.

Stars that glimmer high above,
Keep watch on dreams of old,
As the world is wrapped in silence,
In a blanket fierce and cold.

The moon sings sweet to waiting hearts,
Cradled in the gleam,
Painting all with silver light,
In a perfect dream.

When the morning gently stirs,
With rays of golden light,
Awakens hope from frozen sleep,
Chasing off the night.

Each heart carries a story,
Of the warmth that life can bring,
Through the seasons of our souls,
In this dance of winter's sting.

Beneath the Glaze of Solitude

Beneath the glaze of solitude,
A whisper lingers in the air.
The shadows dance in quietude,
As thoughts drift gently, unaware.

The moon casts silver on the ground,
A shimmering path for the lost.
In silence, there is beauty found,
Yet every peace must bear a cost.

The trees stand tall, with arms outstretched,
Cradling dreams of a fading light.
Each moment felt, each heart enetched,
In time's embrace, both cold and bright.

Beneath the sky's vast, starry dome,
The night wraps dreams in velvet grace.
In solitude, we'll find a home,
Where echoes hold their softest place.

In quiet corners, thoughts reside,
Unraveled tales of fleeting days.
Beneath the glaze, we oft confide,
In solitude's warm, tender gaze.

Lost in the Breath of Winter

Lost in the breath of winter's chill,
Each flake descends like whispered thought.
The world, transformed by silence still,
A canvas bare where warmth is sought.

Barren trees, with limbs outspread,
Cradle dreams of springtime's bloom.
Yet in the frost, new seeds are fed,
Awaiting life to break the gloom.

Footprints carve a path on snow,
As shadows stretch across the night.
In every gust, the cold winds blow,
Embracing hearts in soft respite.

Icicles hang like jeweled tears,
Glistening under moonlit skies.
In frozen breath, we lose our fears,
As winter whispers soft goodbyes.

Lost in the breath, we find our way,
Through chilly winds and frosty air.
Each moment passed, like night to day,
Brings warmth to souls, a solace rare.

Moments Encased in Frost

Moments encased in frost's embrace,
Each sigh a crystal, pure and bright.
Time holds still in icy grace,
A fleeting dream cloaked in white.

The world sleeps under winter's veil,
A hush blankets the earth below.
Each breath forms whispers, soft and pale,
As stars peek down with gentle glow.

Echoes of laughter linger near,
Frozen in time, a sweet refrain.
In every flake, a memory dear,
A tapestry of joy and pain.

Nights stretch long, wrapped in the cold,
While warmth resides within our hearts.
In frost's embrace, tales yet untold,
Await the dawn, where hope restarts.

Moments encased, forever stored,
In nature's chill, our spirits play.
As time drifts on, we feel restored,
In subtle ways, come what may.

Timeless Echoes of the Cold

Timeless echoes of the cold,
Resound in whispers through the trees.
Each breath the night air did enfold,
Carries tales on the chilling breeze.

The stars above, a distant glow,
Illuminate the winter's phase.
In silence, all our wonders flow,
And revere the night's cool praise.

Snowflakes swirl in a ballet light,
Each one unique in its descent.
As shadows lengthen, day turns night,
Beneath the cold, our hearts are lent.

With every heartbeat, echoes ring,
A symphony of frost and fire.
In winter's grasp, our hopes take wing,
As dreams arise and never tire.

Timeless echoes softly sigh,
Resounding in our souls so deep.
In cold embraces, we dare to fly,
As winter keeps its watchful sleep.

Emptiness Wrapped in White

A blanket of silence lies beneath,
The weight of snow is cold and deep.
Footprints vanish in the soft embrace,
Echoes of memories, lost in sleep.

Trees stand still, their branches bare,
Cradling whispers of winter's breath.
In the stillness, a heavy air,
Life held captive, awaiting death.

The horizon melts with shades of gray,
A world transformed, blank canvas vast.
In each flake, a story to say,
Yet all remain untold, unsurpassed.

Loneliness drifts on chilly winds,
Each gust a gentle, sighing plea.
Time moves slow as warmth rescinds,
And all that's left is emptiness, free.

Yet in this void, a beauty finds,
A quiet peace that softly grows.
For in each loss, a thread entwines,
In emptiness, the heart still glows.

Stillness Beneath the Moonlight

In twilight's hush, the world stands still,
The moonlight casts its silver glow.
A gentle peace, a tender thrill,
Awakens thoughts that softly flow.

Beneath the stars, the whispers blend,
With night's embrace, my worries cease.
In shadows deep, my heart may mend,
And find within a sacred peace.

The trees sway slow, a silent dance,
As crickets serenade the night.
Each moment holds a fleeting chance,
To savor joy in soft twilight.

Reflections shimmer on the lake,
A fleeting glimpse of what's to come.
In stillness found, the heart will wake,
To dreams once lost, now gently hum.

Each breath a note in evening's song,
The universe, a lullaby.
With moonlit skies, where I belong,
Stillness wraps the world, and I fly.

Glistening Shadows

In the fading light, shadows play,
Dancing softly, the dusk descends.
Every corner holds a story,
Whispers echo where the daylight ends.

A tapestry woven with subtle hues,
Night paints the world in shades anew.
Glistening stars like scattered clues,
Lead us deeper to shadows' view.

Between the light and dark, they weave,
A fragile line of what is true.
In their embrace, we learn to believe,
That beauty lies in what's unseen too.

Each flicker hints at dreams untold,
Rising softly from the earth below.
In a world of glistening shadows bold,
We find the light that starts to grow.

So let us roam where twilight glows,
Through the canvas where wonders blend.
In glistening shadows, the spirit flows,
With every step, our hearts transcend.

Subtle Haze of Winter's Grip

A breath of chill hangs in the air,
The world adorned in frosted lace.
Winter whispers with a gentle stare,
As everything slows in nature's brace.

The branches bend, encased in white,
A crystal shimmer paints the scene.
Each flake like thoughts lost in the night,
Falling softly, serene and keen.

In the distance, a faint light glows,
Where fires crackle, warmth ignites.
Yet outside, the cold wind blows,
Wrapping the world in winter's sights.

Beneath the sky, a subtle haze,
A quiet ache of beauty stirs.
In frosty air, the heart displays,
The love that lingers, unobserved.

As dawn breaks forth, the light may lift,
Yet winter's grip still holds me tight.
In the subtle haze, there lies a gift,
A moment paused, a cherished rite.

Serenade of the Lone Pine

Underneath the vast, blue sky,
A lone pine sings, and whispers high.
Its needles sway, a soothing song,
Echoing where the heart belongs.

The breeze, it dances through its boughs,
A gentle touch, a silent vow.
With every rustle, nature sighs,
In harmony, the spirit flies.

A melody both soft and bold,
In sunlight warm and shadows cold.
The pine stands tall against the day,
A steadfast friend along the way.

By day it glows in golden light,
By night, it holds the starry sight.
In every season, still it sways,
A timeless tune that never strays.

So let the soccer birds take flight,
While melodies weave through the night.
In every note, a world divine,
The serenade of the lone pine.

Embrace of the Wintry Dusk

As twilight wraps the earth in white,
The dusk descends, a tranquil sight.
Snowflakes whisper, gently fall,
In winter's hush, we hear its call.

Frosty breath upon the air,
Shimmers softly without a care.
The world transforms in silver glow,
Embraced by dusk, the cold winds blow.

The trees stand proud, in crisp array,
Beneath a veil of fading day.
Footprints mark the snow-strewn ground,
In quietude, peace can be found.

As shadows stretch and time stands still,
The heart is warmed, the world fulfilled.
In every flake a story spun,
An embrace shared, two souls as one.

This wintry dusk, a fleeting chance,
We find our rhythm in its dance.
In nature's hand, we find our trust,
In love, we rise—from snow to dust.

Twilight's Shivering Silence

In twilight's glow, silence reigns,
With whispers soft as gentle rains.
The stars awaken, one by one,
As daylight fades, the night begun.

The moon ascends, a silver crest,
In stillness bright, the world finds rest.
Shadows play, as dreams take flight,
In twilight's pause, all feels right.

A moment brief, yet deep with grace,
Where time escapes, we find our place.
In shivering silence, hearts ignite,
Under the canvas painted light.

As night unfolds, the hush enfolds,
We gather secrets, quiet, bold.
In every breath, the world slows down,
In twilight's arms, there's love abound.

So linger long, as stars emerge,
In twilight's end, our souls converge.
Together we tread paths unknown,
In shivering silence, not alone.

Slumber in Snowflakes

Snowflakes whisper soft and light,
Dancing in the glowing night.
They blanket dreams in purest white,
As slumber wraps the world in sight.

Each flake a wish, a fleeting grace,
In winter's hold, we find our place.
The earth lulled under nature's tune,
Under the gaze of the silver moon.

Stars peep down in icy gleam,
While hearts embrace a gentle dream.
In this stillness, troubles fade,
In snowflakes' love, we find our aid.

So let the world go quiet now,
Beneath the snow, we take a bow.
In whispered dreams, our hopes are sown,
In slumber sweet, we feel at home.

Awake refreshed as dawn arrives,
From winter's hush, new spirit thrives.
In every flake, life's beauty glows,
As slumber in snowflakes softly flows.

When Time Hangs in Ice

Moments freeze beneath the sky,
Whispers lost in breath of chill.
Thoughts like snowflakes softly sigh,
Drifting dreams, elusive thrill.

Time stretches taut, a frozen stream,
Echoes linger, soft and light.
Shadows dance on winter's beam,
Stars above in quiet flight.

Heartbeats pulse in silent doubt,
Caught in stillness, endless wait.
Each tick echoes, memories shout,
Frozen hopes, and muted fate.

Stillness holds its cold embrace,
Glimmers of what once had been.
In this world of icy grace,
Time stands still, a timeless scene.

Yet warmth breaks through, a heartbeat's call,
Fires ignite in frozen night.
In the chill, we rise and fall,
Awakening, hearts take flight.

Haunting Reverie of the Frosty Dawn

Morning light creeps in so slow,
Frosty breath upon the air.
Ghostly whispers start to glow,
Memories of warmth laid bare.

Shadows dance on glistening ground,
Echoes from the past return.
Silent songs in dawn are found,
In the light, our spirits yearn.

Each moment fleeting, soft as snow,
Yet haunting in their gentle grace.
Fragments of what we used to know,
Trace the lines on Time's cold face.

Promises in crystals lie,
Fading dreams in pale array.
Underneath the vast, grey sky,
Frost lingers, keeping hope at bay.

Yet in this chilly, hazy sphere,
Love still flickers, still aligns.
Even through the frosty veneer,
Sunrise paints our hearts with signs.

Flickers of a Glistening Dream

Tiny sparkles in the air,
Dancing light on winter's breath.
Glimmers whisper, soft and rare,
Dreams alive, though wrapped in death.

Through the cold, a warmth appears,
Fingers trace the icy streams.
In the stillness, stifled fears,
Flickers glow, igniting dreams.

Moments parked in silver frost,
Years suspended, gently weighed.
In this chill, no love is lost,
Hope remains, though shadows played.

Eyes closed tight, we drift away,
Cocooned in the winter's song.
Flickers guide our hearts to stay,
As the world spins, wild and strong.

Every heartbeat pulses bright,
In the realm of endless night.
Flickers of a dream ignite,
And lead us to the morning light.

Unsung Verses in the Cold

Words unspoken, frozen tight,
Breath of winter, crisp and bold.
Stories linger in the night,
Unsung verses, secrets told.

Echoes weave in branches bare,
Softly whispered through the trees.
Silent songs hang in the air,
Carried gently by the breeze.

Frozen thoughts begin to thaw,
In the light of rising dawn.
Each new day, a hopeful law,
Love like sunlight, never gone.

In this frozen world we tread,
Life continues, beats and flows.
Though it seems like words are dead,
Every heart quietly knows.

Thus we sing our unsung lines,
In the chill, warmth intertwined.
Through the frost, our spirit shines,
In the cold, our love defined.

Serenity in the Frigid Light

A whisper in the winter air,
Silent as a falling star.
The world in gentle stillness rests,
Beneath a chill, a calming spar.

Frosted branches softly gleam,
Wrapped in blankets of pure white.
Nature's breath, a tranquil dream,
Filling hearts with calm delight.

Moonlight dances on the snow,
Casting shadows on the ground.
In this peace, we come to know,
True beauty in silence found.

As the stars begin to fade,
And dawn breaks in pastel glow,
All worries, fears cascade,
In serenity's warm flow.

Moments pass in gentle sighs,
Time suspended in this place.
In the frigid light, we rise,
Embracing grace, a soft embrace.

Crystalline Canvas of Allurement

In the hush of winter's breath,
A canvas shines, untouched by beat.
Crystalline patterns weave their path,
Beauty laid beneath our feet.

Diamond dew on grass does cling,
Glistening under early sun.
Every sparkle, bright as spring,
Nature's art has just begun.

Captured light in icy forms,
Creating worlds that mesmerize.
A dance of flakes, a flurry swarms,
Awakening our wonder's eyes.

With each gust, the landscape shifts,
New patterns born within the cold.
This dance of nature, endless gifts,
Stories of silence yet untold.

As night falls, the crystals glow,
Imbued with magic, soft and bright.
In this wonder, hearts may know,
The allure of winter's light.

The Depth of the Stillness

In the depths of winter's night,
Stillness wraps the world so tight.
Every sound, a distant dream,
In this peace, we find our theme.

Frozen lakes, reflections deep,
Capture stars in silent sleep.
An echo of all that was,
In stillness, we pause, just because.

The trees stand tall, a solemn guard,
Holding secrets, hushed and hard.
In their silence, wisdom lies,
A testament against the skies.

Time unmoving as the snow,
Every flake, a story's flow.
Beneath the surface, life holds sway,
In this quiet, we drift away.

As dawn breaks with gentle light,
Awakening the heart's delight.
The depth of stillness whispers clear,
Life's embrace is always near.

Fading Footprints Across the Frost

Each step made in morning glow,
Leaves behind a trace so light.
Fading footprints on the snow,
A journey lost to winter's bite.

Wisps of breath in frosted air,
Tell a tale of wandering hearts.
Tracks that vanish, fragile, rare,
Stories end as silence starts.

Nature's canvas, pure and wide,
Marks of passage, soon erased.
In the quiet, we confide,
Fleeting moments softly paced.

As the sun begins to climb,
Shadows stretch, the shapes do shift.
In the dance of passing time,
Life reminds us of its gift.

In crusted snow, we tread again,
Holding memories held so dear.
Though the footprints fade like rain,
In our hearts, they linger near.

Whispers of Frost

In the dawn's soft light, whispers arise,
Frosty breath dances 'neath azure skies.
Silent tales weave through the chilly air,
Nature's secrets linger, everywhere.

Each blade of grass, a jeweled delight,
Captured in crystals, glimmering bright.
The world holds its breath, a serene expanse,
In whispers of frost, we find our chance.

Trees stand adorned in a silvered grace,
Framed by the stillness, a tranquil space.
Echoes of winter, gentle and clear,
In the morning hush, they beckon near.

Footsteps crunch softly on pathways so white,
Where shadows embrace the fading light.
In the fleeting moments, dreams start to beat,
In whispers of frost, hearts find their heat.

As sunlight rises, the frost starts to weep,
Dripping like secrets from slumbering sleep.
Yet memories linger, wrapped in the chill,
In whispers of frost, time stands still.

Echoes in the Stillness

In the quiet of night, a soft refrain,
Echoes of stillness, a soothing pain.
Stars whisper secrets to the moon's glow,
Guiding lost souls to the warmth below.

Crickets are singing their lullaby tune,
While shadows enchant under the watchful moon.
Time holds its breath, an exquisite pause,
In echoes of stillness, we find our cause.

Beneath towering pines, silence takes form,
Wrapped in the arms of a gentle storm.
Thoughts drift like clouds, float away the strife,
In echoes of stillness, we savor life.

Rustling leaves share tales from the past,
Of dreams that linger, of shadows cast.
The night paints a canvas, soft and deep,
In echoes of stillness, our spirits leap.

As dawn breaks anew, whispers take flight,
Echoes fade gently, welcoming light.
But the memories crafted in night's embrace,
In echoes of stillness, leave their trace.

Frost's Quiet Embrace

A silver cloak rests on the world so wide,
Frost's quiet embrace, nature's soft pride.
Morning unfolds in a shimmer of light,
Wrapped in a hush, everything feels right.

Branches now sparkle, a jeweled display,
In the still of the morn, night fades away.
Footsteps are muffled on pathways of white,
In frost's quiet embrace, peace is in sight.

The breath of the earth, crystal and clear,
Holds stories of winter, for those who hear.
A delicate touch on each leaf and stone,
In frost's quiet embrace, we're never alone.

Clouds drift like whispers across the blue sky,
Veiling the sunlight; it dims—but won't die.
Nature's cool fingers, like lace, interlace,
In frost's quiet embrace, we find our place.

With every sunrise, the frost bids adieu,
Yet memories linger, fresh—like the dew.
Though winter may fade, its beauty won't race,
In frost's quiet embrace, we always find space.

Shivers of the Night

As dusk falls softly, the chill takes flight,
Casting long shadows, shivers of night.
The wind's gentle sighs weave tales through the trees,
Whispers of winter dance on the breeze.

Stars spark like diamonds on velvet so deep,
While the world beneath wraps itself in sleep.
Crickets will sing, their lullabies bright,
Under the shimmer of shivers of night.

The moon hangs low, a lantern so pale,
Guiding the dreamers along hidden trails.
Each heartbeat echoed in stillness so right,
In the embrace of soft shivers of night.

Thoughts travel far on the wings of the breeze,
Wandering realms where the heart finds its ease.
Silence invites with its soothing delight,
In realms of shadow, the shivers ignite.

Yet dawn will approach, with a warm, tender glow,
Chasing the whispers, the chill will let go.
But memories linger, soft as starlight,
In the heart's quiet dance, shivers of night.

A World Clad in Hibernation

The trees stand bare and silent,
Blanketed in frost, they wait.
Patches of ice gleam softly,
Nature's breath held, still, sedate.

Moonlight dances on the drifts,
Shadows play in silver hues.
Creatures dream beneath the earth,
Wrapped in slumber, hidden cues.

Chill winds whisper through the boughs,
Ancient songs of seasons past.
Time slows down in winter's grasp,
A world untouched, serene, steadfast.

The stars are bright, yet distant,
Crystals cling to every branch.
In this moment, all is calm,
A cradle sways—a gentle ranch.

Yet beneath, life stirs and swells,
Waiting for the sun's warm touch.
Dreams of spring are softly spun,
In winter's arms, we linger much.

Ghosts Beneath the Snow

Silent whispers in the night,
Echoes of the lives before.
Footsteps lost in powdered white,
Memories etched on frozen floor.

Shadows dance with the moonlight,
As the world slips into dreams.
Haunting tales of love and loss,
Woven in the silent seams.

Figures drift like evening mist,
Faces pale, with stories told.
In the chill, their laughter sings,
Ghosts of warmth, in depths of cold.

Beneath the snow, they linger long,
With each flake, a sigh and tear.
In the quiet, they belong,
Resting close, forever near.

As dawn breaks, they fade away,
Remnants of the night's embrace.
Yet their whispers gently stay,
Carried forth, time can't erase.

Still Waters Run Cold

Where the river lays frozen,
Beneath the still and silent ice.
Secrets hidden, deep and old,
In the depths, the world's precise.

Reflections dance on surface clear,
Fractured images merge and part.
A shimmer of what once was near,
Lost in winter's steadfast heart.

Time is stilled, as if in prayer,
The world awaits a thawing sun.
With every glance, a quiet stare,
As if to hear what's left undone.

Nature's breath is crisp as glass,
In the hollow of the dawn.
Where the shadows softly pass,
Still the waters, life goes on.

And beneath that icy shield,
Dreams of spring do softly swell.
For beneath stillness, life is sealed,
Waiting for the bell to knell.

Tranquil Nights of the Cold

In the hush of evening's cradle,
Stars alert, their watch to keep.
Blankets of frost on every table,
Nature hushed, in quiet sleep.

The moon hangs bright, a silver globe,
Casting spells on frozen ground.
Gentle winds in whispers probe,
Lost in dreams, no thoughts are found.

Candles flicker, shadows dance,
In the corners, memories play.
Cocoa warms with every glance,
While the chill fades far away.

Wrapped up tight in layers warm,
Embers glow with tales of light.
Tranquility becomes the norm,
Life slows down, embraced by night.

In these hours, time is soft,
And peace surrounds in every fold.
A world asleep, aloft,
In tranquil nights of the cold.

Bygone Whispers of the Wind

In the dusk where shadows creep,
Old secrets whisper, silence deep.
Leaves flutter soft, a gentle sigh,
Echoes of laughter that once passed by.

Time drifts like smoke from a fire,
Carrying tales of lost desire.
Reflections fade in twilight's grace,
Memories linger, a sweet embrace.

Now the stillness fills the air,
Winds weave stories, love and care.
Beneath the stars, where dreams reside,
Bygone whispers shall abide.

Hearts once brave now turn to dust,
Yet in the whispers, there's still trust.
The night carries the ache, the thrill,
In every rustle, every chill.

So let the wind take all away,
And guard the past till the break of day.
In journey's end, we find our peace,
In bygone whispers, joys increase.

Crystal Veins of Solitude

In the quiet corners of the night,
Heartbeats linger, soft and light.
Lonely echoes in silence bloom,
Crystal veins of unspoken gloom.

Dreams thread through a hollow space,
Their shimmering edges, a delicate lace.
In solitude, we dance alone,
Finding solace in the unknown.

A single tear glistens bright,
With every shimmer, a fleeting light.
Walls surround, yet thoughts take flight,
In crystal veins, our fears ignite.

Time pauses in the stillness here,
Filled with hope, yet touched with fear.
A whisper calls, both near and far,
Guiding souls beneath the stars.

In the depths where shadows lie,
Glimmers of courage softly sigh.
Through crystal veins, we weave our fate,
In solitude, we resonate.

Ghosts of a Frigid Hour

Beneath a shroud of silver mist,
Ghosts emerge from time's dark twist.
Whispers dance on icy breath,
In the shadows, the echoes of death.

Each fleeting shape, a memory lost,
In the quiet, we pay the cost.
Frigid air wraps around our skin,
As the past stirs, the haunt begins.

Through frozen fields, we chase the light,
Yet find only shadows in the night.
A spectral touch brushes our cheek,
In this hour, the silence speaks.

The clock ticks down, the world stands still,
Ghosts of heartache, sorrow to fill.
Memories flicker like candle flames,
Calling our hearts with whispered names.

In this frigid hour, we embrace the cold,
Tales of yesteryears slowly unfold.
For even in darkness, shadows find grace,
Ghosts linger softly, time cannot erase.

Breathless in the Cold

In the stillness where snowflakes waltz,
Breathless moments weave with faults.
Each inhale sharp, the air so clear,
Whispering dreams we hold so dear.

Frozen landscapes stretch and bend,
Time moves slowly, no need to pretend.
Every heartbeat, a soft refrain,
In the cold, we break the chain.

Chasing shadows, we heed the call,
Under the weight of winter's thrall.
In bright white, our spirits roam,
Finding warmth in our heart's home.

The quiet speaks, a lover's breath,
Wraps us tight, a dance with death.
Yet through the chill, we dare to hold,
Each moment sacred, fiercely bold.

So here we stand, breathless and free,
In the cold, we find unity.
Through frost and ice, love will ignite,
Forever warmed by shared light.

Chilling Embrace of Stillness

In the quiet night, all is calm,
The world wrapped in a frozen balm.
Stars twinkle softly in the sky,
As whispers of the wind gently sigh.

The trees stand tall, their branches bare,
Beneath a moonlight's silvery glare.
Snowflakes dance, a delicate show,
In a serene land, where dreams flow.

A hush blankets the earth so wide,
In chilling embrace, nature's pride.
Time slows down, the heart stands still,
Wrapped in peace, a tranquil thrill.

With every breath, the cold air sings,
Of winter's touch, and all it brings.
In this stillness, we find our place,
Embraced by time, in nature's grace.

Here in the silence, we pause to think,
Of moments lost, and dreams on the brink.
The night whispers secrets, hushed and deep,
In the chilling embrace, where souls do keep.

Subdued Whispers in the Dark

In shadows deep, where silence reigns,
Subdued whispers carry soft refrains.
The night cradles thoughts, gentle and shy,
As secrets unfold with a tender sigh.

Moonlight filters through branches thin,
Bathe in the glow, let the stillness begin.
Echoes of stories from ages past,
Weaving through dreams, a spell is cast.

The dark holds a magic, unseen yet bright,
In every corner, a flicker of light.
Voices so soft, they shimmer and fall,
A symphony hushed, for those who call.

Time drifts slowly, like the shadows around,
In subdued whispers, mysteries abound.
Embrace the silence and let it be,
For the dark holds a world, wild and free.

In every heartbeat, a tale is spun,
Of hope in the shadows, where all are one.
So breathe in the calm, let the whispers flow,
In the depth of the night, let your spirit grow.

Glimmers of Light on Frozen Paths

Frosted trails underfoot we tread,
Chasing the glimmers that warmly spread.
Each step reveals a radiant gleam,
Guiding our hearts like a waking dream.

Icicles hanging, like chandeliers bright,
Sparkling treasures in the soft twilight.
Paths once obscured now clearly show,
The beauty of winter, where wonders grow.

Beneath the bright stars, we wander free,
Lost in the magic of what we see.
Nature's canvas, with strokes so bold,
Radiant whispers, stories untold.

With every flicker in the cold night air,
Hope ignites, dispelling despair.
Footprints shimmer on the frozen ground,
A dance of light where love is found.

In the stillness, our spirits blend,
Following glimmers, where journeys extend.
Through frozen paths, hearts intertwine,
In the glow of light, our souls align.

Unseen Footsteps in the Snow

A pristine blanket, white as the dawn,
The world transformed, as night feels drawn.
Footsteps hidden, where no one goes,
Secrets held tight, in whispers of snow.

Silent silhouettes weave in the cold,
Each corner turned, a story told.
Wind dances softly, through branches bare,
Unseen footsteps linger, light as air.

In the stillness, echoes softly play,
Carried away, like dusk into day.
Mysteries beckon in the crisp night air,
Footprints of dreams, linger everywhere.

The chill embraces, a gentle hold,
In the silence deep, courage unfolds.
With each unseen stride, a path we forge,
In the snowy depths, where dreams emerge.

Winter's canvas, untouched and pure,
Unseen footsteps whisper, we are secure.
In this moment, find your peace,
As the snowflakes dance, let worries cease.

Echoes of a Sunken World

Beneath the waves, a whisper calls,
In shadows deep, a silence falls.
Forgotten dreams, in depths they lie,
Where time stands still, and moments die.

Ghostly ships, now turned to ghost,
Adrift on tides, they lost their post.
Echoes of laughter, now turned gray,
In the ocean's grip, they drift away.

Faded maps of lands once bold,
Now tales of sorrow silently told.
Where mermaids sing to midnight's veil,
In watery graves, their hearts now sail.

Bubbles rise from sunken clay,
Ancient secrets ebb and sway.
The moonlight dances on the deep,
Guarding dreams that time can't keep.

In the darkness, hope still gleams,
For echoes linger in forgotten dreams.
A sunken world with tales to share,
Forever lost, yet always there.

Silence Lingers on Frostbitten Paths

Beneath the chill, the silence reigns,
As frostbite whispers through the grains.
Footsteps echo on the snowy white,
Where shadows blend with fading light.

Amidst the trees, a secret lies,
Where winter wraps the world in sighs.
Each breath a cloud, each pause a dream,
As silence weaves its gentle theme.

The icy wind, a haunting song,
In frozen realms where time is long.
Nature sleeps in a quilt of snow,
Yet deep within, the embers glow.

Twilight falls on desolate trails,
Where hope persists, despite the gales.
A gentle touch of sun awaited,
In silence, beauty's softly gated.

As moonlight glimmers on the cold,
Stories of old begin to unfold.
In frozen worlds, we find our path,
Embraced by nature's gentle wrath.

Crystallized Words Lost to the Wind

In the quiet place where whispers lie,
Crystallized words drift and sigh.
Carried forth on gusts unseen,
They weave a tale in spaces between.

Fragments of thought, like shards of glass,
Twinkling softly as they pass.
Each syllable, a fleeting glance,
In the dance of fate's own chance.

A poet's heart, once bold and bright,
Now echoes lost in fading light.
For every word that dared to roam,
Is bound to wander far from home.

The breeze a thief, in playful jest,
Stealing meanings, leaving rest.
Yet in the air, they still reside,
Awaiting souls to seek and guide.

In every gust, a story wakes,
A melody the moment makes.
Though lost in time, they swirl and spin,
Crystallized words, forever thin.

Still Echoes of the Frozen Earth

In whispers low, the earth lays still,
Wrapped in silence, a magic thrill.
Each flake of snow, a gentle touch,
Reminds us that we feel so much.

Frozen lakes with mirrored skies,
Reflecting dreams in lullabies.
The world a canvas, stark and bright,
In winter's grasp, a pure delight.

Echoes linger in the frosty air,
A soft reminder of love and care.
The crunch of footsteps, sharp and clear,
Guides us through the path we fear.

Bare branches reach for stars above,
In the stillness, we find our love.
Each frozen breath, a fleeting tease,
Carried onward by the chill breeze.

In this quiet, hearts entwine,
In the echoes of a world divine.
For even in the coldest night,
Hope is born in soft twilight.

Silent Dance of Snowfall

Snowflakes fall in gentle grace,
Whispering secrets, soft embrace.
The world adorned in shimmering white,
Silent dance through the night.

Branches bow with frosty weight,
Each flake a dream, a whispered fate.
Twinkling lights in distant view,
Nature's magic, fresh and new.

Footprints trace a fleeting path,
In winter's charm, we feel its wrath.
But hearts are warm, as fires glow,
In the silent dance of snow.

Every flake a fleeting song,
A moment's peace, where we belong.
As moonlight bathes the icy ground,
In this stillness, dreams are found.

The world awaits the dawn's first light,
In this tranquil, snowy night.
A canvas pure, untouched and free,
Reflecting life's simplicity.

Frigid Air and Whispered Dreams

Biting winds weave through the trees,
Carrying whispers of the freeze.
Stars are scattered, bright and clear,
In the night, we draw near.

Breath hangs heavy, cloud-like puffs,
In the chill, the soul rebuffs.
Yet in the cold, we find a spark,
A warmth ignites within the dark.

Echoes linger, soft and sly,
Holding secrets of the sky.
In every gust, a tale unfolds,
Of ancient dreams and futures bold.

Frigid air wraps us tight,
Guarding dreams through the night.
As frost paints all in silver hues,
We hush our hearts to hear the cues.

A world renewed in frosty breath,
In whispers feels a kind of death.
But life persists, a quiet hum,
In frigid air, our thoughts become.

Harbinger of the Frosty Night

Night descends with a icy veil,
Moonlight gleams like a silver trail.
The harbinger of frost draws near,
In shadows, all we hold dear.

Crisp air crackles, scents of pine,
Whispers linger, secrets entwine.
Trees stand tall, a watchful guard,
As silence blankets paths so hard.

A chill creeps in, wraps us close,
In frosty whispers, longing grows.
With every heartbeat, dreams take flight,
In the magic of the night.

Stars above begin to twinkle,
In this stillness, hearts can wrinkle.
Each moment swells with quiet grace,
A chance to find our sacred place.

The frost displays its crystal art,
A tender touch upon the heart.
In the night, dreams softly bloom,
In the harbinger, we find room.

Shadows in the Stillness

In the stillness, shadows play,
Dancing softly, night meets day.
Every whisper, every breath,
Holds the promise of life's depth.

Moon casts shadows, long and thin,
Through the trees, where dreams begin.
Footsteps echo, soft and slow,
In the dark, the heart can grow.

Nighttime cradles, gently sways,
Encouraging the mind to stray.
In shadows deep, secrets lie,
Waiting softly for a sigh.

As silence wraps the world around,
In shadows lost, we are found.
Moments linger, time stands still,
In the quiet, we feel the thrill.

Beneath the stars, where dreams convene,
In shadows soft, life's touch is seen.
In stillness deep, our spirits rise,
Embracing whispers of the skies.

Starlight in a Frozen Breath

A shimmer dances in the night,
Whispers of dreams take gentle flight.
Each spark a wish on icy air,
Fleeting hopes beyond despair.

The world is wrapped in silver sheen,
Echoes of laughter, softly seen.
Crystals hang on branches bare,
A moment caught, exquisite, rare.

In this stillness, time stands still,
Every heartbeat a tranquil thrill.
Underneath the cobalt sky,
Stars awaken, softly sigh.

Breath of cold, a tender kiss,
Frosty echoes, a whisper's bliss.
Nature's tune, a quiet song,
Guiding lost souls where they belong.

In twilight's grip, the magic weaves,
A tapestry of winter leaves.
Hand in hand, we'll trace the light,
Together beneath the grateful night.

Threads of a Chilling Peace

In the quiet of the evening chill,
Moonlight weaves a tapestry still.
Softly wrapped in a dreamlike haze,
Nature bows in a reverent gaze.

Whispers linger, secrets shared,
In this silence, no one's scared.
Each breath taken, a thread spun tight,
Binding hearts through the winter night.

Stars like stitches in vastness wide,
Embroider stories that never hide.
The chill holds close what warmth we find,
As peace entwines, our souls aligned.

Winds of change, they softly blow,
Bringing solace from the snow.
In every flake, a tale retold,
Of laughter, love, and hearts so bold.

So let the night spread its embrace,
With gentle hands, a tender grace.
In threads of peace, we'll find our way,
Together, warmed by shared array.

Moonlit Silence on Frost's Edge

Beneath the moon's enchanting glow,
A realm of silence wrapped in snow.
Frosty whispers float through the night,
Calling for dreams to take their flight.

Each step echoes a longing tune,
As shadows dance beneath the moon.
With every breath, the world seems new,
And serenity lingers, calm and true.

The frost's edge glimmers in the light,
A fragile world, ethereal sight.
Branches bow with snowflakes crowned,
In this stillness, peace is found.

Time slows down in silver beams,
Wrapped in quiet, lost in dreams.
Nature hums a gentle song,
Reminding us where we belong.

So let us wander through the night,
In moonlit silence, pure delight.
Hand in hand, where warmth is near,
Together, casting away the fear.

Imprints of a Weary Heart

Each tread we take leaves marks of strain,
Imprints made through joy and pain.
The heart, though heavy, still beats strong,
In shadows cast, we still belong.

Navigating through paths unknown,
With every tear, a seed has grown.
In weary nights and hopeful dawns,
Resilience lives where love carries on.

Through trials faced, we find our way,
In whispers of hope, we choose to stay.
The scars we bear, they tell our tale,
Of battles fought, we will prevail.

Let the silence cradle our fears,
For every laugh has birthed the tears.
In the fabric of time, love's design,
Weaving comfort, one thread at a time.

So as we walk these haunted streets,
Remember, dear, the warmth that greets.
For in the journey, love is art,
Each step we take, an imprint heart.

Frosted Memories of Solitude

In the quiet of the morn,
A whisper on the breeze,
Memories dance softly,
Wrapped in frozen leaves.

Footsteps trace the silence,
Through valleys draped in white,
Shadows linger like secrets,
In the fading light.

Snowflakes drift like wishes,
Carrying tales of old,
Each flake a breath of winter,
A story yet untold.

Windows frost with longing,
As the world outside sleeps,
Frosted dreams held tight,
In the silence, it keeps.

In this realm of solitude,
Time gently stands still,
A heart wrapped in stillness,
Breathes an echoing thrill.

Veils of White Over Silent Fields

Veils of white descend softly,
Blanketing the earth wide,
Silent fields lie spectating,
While day whispers goodbye.

The distant trees are still now,
Dripping pearls of frost,
Their branches cradle dreams,
Of warmth that we have lost.

Footsteps crunch in the stillness,
Mapping paths in the snow,
Each print tells a story,
Of where hearts dared to go.

Clouds weave a tale above us,
As stars blink from afar,
Night wraps us in its secrets,
Under the crescent star.

As dawn breaks the silence,
The fields awaken new,
Veils of white slowly melt,
Revealing life's sweet hue.

Echoes of a Breathless Night

Under the cloak of starlight,
Night whispers her soft song,
Echoes of tranquility,
In the dark where dreams belong.

The moon holds its secrets,
Casting shadows long and deep,
While the world is lost in slumber,
Wrapped in a tender sleep.

Time flows like a river,
In this breathless embrace,
Every heartbeat a whisper,
In the night's gentle lace.

Winds sing through the branches,
A lullaby so sweet,
Carrying hopes and wishes,
On soft, silvered feet.

In every fleeting moment,
The stillness holds us tight,
Echoes of tomorrow,
In this breathless night.

Eternal Winter's Soft Lament

In the cradle of stillness,
Winter sighs her soft tune,
A lament for the seasons,
Under the watchful moon.

Each breath forms a vision,
A fleeting dance in the air,
Whispers of time forgotten,
Linger gentle and rare.

Frozen rivers reflecting,
The silence of the year,
Carrying tales of longing,
That only hearts can hear.

Flakes fall like soft sorrows,
Covering all with grace,
A tapestry of longing,
In winter's cold embrace.

Eternal winter listens,
To the world's hushed refrain,
In every flake of snow,
Lies a soft, sweet pain.

Shivers in the Air

Cold winds wrap around me tight,
Breath visible in the fading light.
Leaves dance down from trees so bare,
A gentle chill—a shiver in the air.

Moonlight glimmers on frozen ground,
Footsteps echo without a sound.
Stars above, they twinkle and stare,
A quiet night—a shiver in the air.

Winter's whisper through branches spreads,
Nature sleeps in her snowy beds.
The world is still, the night is rare,
A calming hush—a shiver in the air.

As shadows stretch across the land,
I feel the coldness take my hand.
With every breath, I'm caught in despair,
But there's a beauty—a shiver in the air.

In this season, dreams take flight,
In icy realms of silver light.
A fleeting moment, I stop and stare,
Embracing wonder—a shiver in the air.

A Canvas of Ice

The world transformed, a sheet so bright,
Glistening softly in morning light.
Each curve and edge, nature's design,
A stunning work—a canvas of ice.

Patterns etched by winter's hand,
A fragile beauty across the land.
Every breath creates a new slice,
A masterpiece—this canvas of ice.

Icicles hang from eaves like glass,
Reflecting moments as they pass.
Nature's artwork, cool and precise,
Forever changing—this canvas of ice.

Beneath the chill, life waits in peace,
Anticipating spring's warm release.
A frozen pause, an exquisite vice,
A fleeting gem—this canvas of ice.

With each gentle thaw, colors ignite,
The world awakens, shedding the night.
Yet memories linger, crisp and nice,
Forever cherished—this canvas of ice.

Whispers of Bare Branches

Silent woods stand stark and bare,
Whispers float lightly through the air.
Nature sighs, each branch a prayer,
In the stillness—whispers of bare branches.

The frost coats limbs, a crystal lace,
In shadows deep, there's quiet grace.
A symphony soft, a gentle affair,
Subtle secrets—whispers of bare branches.

As dusk arrives, the world grows dim,
A haunting tune from the twilight whim.
Each rustle speaks of stories rare,
Echoing softly—whispers of bare branches.

Amidst the cold, life stirs below,
A promise held in the silent glow.
Hope lingers long, a brave debonair,
In the murmurs—whispers of bare branches.

Seasons will shift, rebirth will come,
Yet now we bask in winter's hum.
In every flicker, there's love to share,
Life's gentle murmur—whispers of bare branches.

Shroud of Silence Over Fields

Fields lie quiet, wrapped in white,
A shroud of silence claims the night.
Each wayward breeze begins to weave,
A tranquil spell—a shroud of silence over fields.

Stars twinkle faintly, glimmers divine,
Moonlight spills where shadows entwine.
In this stillness, hearts believe,
In peace found here—a shroud of silence over fields.

The frost-kissed grass whispers its tale,
Of dreams once vibrant, now pale.
With nature's breath, we take our leave,
To dance in calm—a shroud of silence over fields.

As night embraces the sleeping land,
Time stands still, simple and grand.
In every heartbeat, we perceive,
The beauty held—a shroud of silence over fields.

When dawn awakens, softly it yields,
Life returns with the warmth it wields.
Yet, in the memory, we retrieve,
The magic woven—a shroud of silence over fields.

Chasing Shadows of an Icy Dawn

In the quiet, shadows creep,
Frosty whispers break the deep.
Sunrise colors, pale and drawn,
Chasing shadows of an icy dawn.

Footsteps crunch on frozen ground,
Where silence swirls, lost and found.
Nature holds her breath, forlorn,
Chasing shadows of an icy dawn.

Branches glisten, glinting light,
Echoes fade in morning's flight.
Dreams of warmth, the heart's own brawn,
Chasing shadows of an icy dawn.

A feathered friend takes to the air,
Winter's chill is everywhere.
Yet hope emerges, soft and warm,
Chasing shadows of an icy dawn.

With each step, the world awakes,
In the shimmer, the cold shakes.
A new day's promise silently born,
Chasing shadows of an icy dawn.

Whispered Grief of the Cold Sky

Under a blanket of clouded grey,
Silent tears fall where they may.
The cold sky weeps without refrain,
Whispered grief in a soft refrain.

Each droplet holds a nameless tale,
Love once bright, now frail and pale.
Vanished dreams, like whispers, wane,
Whispered grief in a soft refrain.

The wind carries sorrows untold,
Through barren branches, stark and bold.
As shadows dance, we mourn the lane,
Whispered grief in a soft refrain.

Time lingers on a frosted breath,
Moments captured, echoing death.
In twilight's embrace, we feel the strain,
Whispered grief in a soft refrain.

Yet even in the depths of night,
Stars shine softly, a soothing light.
Through loss, a flicker shall remain,
Whispered grief in a soft refrain.

Through a Lens of Ice

Frosted panes distort the view,
Every sight, a glistening hue.
Captured moments freeze in time,
Through a lens of ice, sublime.

Nature wears her frosty crown,
Beauty cloaked in silvery gown.
A world transformed, still, divine,
Through a lens of ice, sublime.

Crystals dance as sunlight glows,
A fleeting glimpse, as the heart knows.
Life encapsulated, pure and fine,
Through a lens of ice, sublime.

Yet behind each perfect sheen,
Lie stories lost, once seen.
Fractured dreams, a fragile line,
Through a lens of ice, sublime.

So we gaze, both near and far,
Finding warmth in the cold's bizarre.
Embracing all that intertwines,
Through a lens of ice, sublime.

Memories Wrapped in Fleece

In winter's hold, where dreams reside,
Memories wrap us, warm and wide.
Fleece cocooned, we find our peace,
Memories wrapped in fleece, a sweet release.

The crackling fire, its tender glow,
Holds every laughter, every flow.
In the silence, time's gentle tease,
Memories wrapped in fleece, a sweet release.

Snowflakes whisper on windowpanes,
Binding moments, love remains.
In soft embrace, our fears appease,
Memories wrapped in fleece, a sweet release.

Through quiet nights and starry skies,
A woven tapestry of sighs.
Among the warmth, the heart agrees,
Memories wrapped in fleece, a sweet release.

Though seasons change and life's a race,
In tender warmth, we find our place.
With every heartbeat, joy's unease,
Memories wrapped in fleece, a sweet release.

The Breath Between Seasons

In whispers of the wind, a change,
Leaves flutter down, a gentle range.
The sun dips low, a fleeting glow,
As twilight dances, softly slow.

Branches shiver, clad in frost,
Memories linger, love not lost.
Within the pause, a delicate sigh,
Nature holds secrets, waiting to fly.

The sky blushes with a painter's hand,
And dreams awaken from silent land.
Colors blend, a sweet embrace,
In the breath between, we find our place.

With every step on crunchy ground,
Hope whispers softly, all around.
In the chill, warmth starts to bloom,
As seasons shift, dispelling gloom.

The world holds its breath, a fleeting grace,
In each tender moment, we find our space.
For in between, there's magic untold,
As life unfolds in hues of gold.

Quiet Corners of the Icy World

In the hush of snow, a secret sleeps,
Softly cradled where silence keeps.
Crystal corners, shadows appear,
Whispers carried through frosty air.

Under the blanket, a soft embrace,
Nature's canvas, pure and chaste.
Footprints linger, fleeting and light,
As day bows down to the approaching night.

Icicles hang like delicate art,
Each glimmering shard a beat of the heart.
While stars twinkle in velvet grey,
Guiding the lost on their wandering way.

A breath of wind stirs the deep,
In quiet corners, secrets we keep.
The stillness holds an age-old song,
In icy realms where we belong.

Time stands still in this frosty embrace,
As nature spins in an elegant chase.
The world, adorned in a diamond sheen,
Finds peace in the spaces so rarely seen.

A Horizon Wrapped in White

Beyond the vale, where dreams can soar,
A horizon beckons, forever more.
Wrapped in white, a snowy veil,
A tranquil vision, a whispered tale.

Mountains greet the sky with pride,
Cloaked in winter where secrets hide.
With every flake, a story unfurls,
In the dance of silence, the heart twirls.

The sun peeks through, a timid glow,
Painting shadows on the glistening snow.
Nature's canvas, vast and bright,
Calls to the wanderer, day and night.

In the stillness, horizons blend,
A meeting of sky and earth, no end.
In white wrapped spaces, dreams take flight,
As hope ignites in the fading light.

With each step forward, a promise we find,
In this snowy realm, wonderfully kind.
A horizon awaits, as moments entwine,
In the beauty of white, our spirits align.

Distant Dreams on Frozen Waves

On frozen waves where stillness reigns,
Whispers of warmth cradle the pains.
Dreams drift lightly as snowflakes fall,
Echoes ripple in the twilight's call.

Beneath the surface, a dance concealed,
A world of wonders, silently healed.
Tales of the deep, whispered by frost,
In transient moments, we are not lost.

Stars above, like lanterns bright,
Guide distant dreams through the quiet night.
With every gust, we chase the spark,
As echoes linger in the frozen dark.

To leap upon surfaces, fleeting and thin,
Embrace the beauty of each destined spin.
For in the distance, we find our way,
On frozen waves where dreams softly sway.

Hope glimmers as horizons call,
In the heart of winter, we rise and fall.
With each passing moment, our spirits blaze,
Among distant dreams on frozen waves.

Murmurs of the Frosted Moon

In silver light, the soft winds sigh,
As shadows dance beneath the sky.
Frosted whispers weave through trees,
Carried gently by the freeze.

Stars twinkle like diamonds bright,
While dreams take flight in winter's night.
Each breath of cold, a silent tune,
Echoing from the frosted moon.

The world is wrapped in a soft embrace,
Nature dons her crystalline grace.
In this calm, a magic brews,
A tapestry of silver hues.

With every heartbeat, the night holds dear,
The shivers of joy, the hints of fear.
Underneath the tranquil gloom,
Life stirs gently in the bloom.

Waves of silence, soft and deep,
Cradle the dreams the night will keep.
In murmurs hush, the night proceeds,
To sow the hopes of future seeds.

Breathless Whispers of the Abyss

In depths where shadows softly creep,
The heart of silence begins to weep.
Ghostly echoes, distant calls,
Breathless whispers down the walls.

Glimmers fade in a shrouded glow,
Time stands still in currents slow.
Lost in the vast, the spirit roams,
Searching softly for its homes.

The ocean's tongue, both dark and deep,
Holds secrets buried, dreams to keep.
In murky waters gently swayed,
Life's essence swirls, forever laid.

Tempting fate with every plunge,
The heart entwined, a breathless lunge.
Each whisper wraps a tale to tell,
Of echoing depths where mysteries dwell.

Moments hang in the chilling air,
Between the worlds, a lingering flare.
In timeless gloom, the dark permits,
A dance of shadows, endless sits.

Melancholy Beneath the Ice

A blanket soft, a crystal sheet,
Hides the world in a still retreat.
Beneath the frost, the heartbeats thud,
In silence deep, a frozen flood.

Memories trapped in layers thick,
Stories whisper, time moves quick.
Brittle branches, frail and bare,
Sway with sorrows in the air.

The sun, a ghost in winter's glare,
Leaves the day with a quiet stare.
Shadows linger, under veils,
As twilight wanes, and daylight pales.

Each sigh of wind, a pained refrain,
Stirring echoes of forgotten pain.
In melancholic, icy dance,
The heart remembers, lost in trance.

Yet even in this bitter cold,
Whispers of warmth and hope unfold.
For underneath the winter's guise,
Life waits, dreaming to arise.

The Quiet Call of the Winter Woods

In the hush of snow, the forest sleeps,
Where secrets dwell, and silence keeps.
Every branch, a tale untold,
Wrapped in whispers, soft and bold.

Footsteps muffled by the snow,
Each step a dance, a gentle flow.
The pine trees sway, a graceful bow,
To winds that whisper, here and now.

Moonlight spills like molten glass,
Upon the ground, as shadows pass.
Crickets hum their waning tunes,
Underneath the watchful moons.

A tranquil call, so deep and wide,
Invites the heart to step inside.
In winter's woods, the spirit finds,
A quiet solace for weary minds.

So linger close, where silence reigns,
And feel the pulse of nature's veins.
Amid the pines, a promise stirs,
Of spring to come, as winter blurs.

The Quietness Beneath Layers of Ice

Beneath the frost, whispers linger,
Silent secrets held in time,
Frozen dreams beneath the shimmer,
Nature's breath, a gentle rhyme.

Icicles hang like crystal tears,
Each one tells a tale of still,
Moments frozen through the years,
In the quiet, time stands still.

The world outside, a muted hue,
Wrapped in blankets, cold and pure,
Yet beneath, life stirs anew,
Hidden warmth, a soft allure.

Echoes dance in glacial air,
Echoing all that's lost and found,
Delicate sighs in frozen glare,
Peaceful, soft, and profound.

Winter's song, a silent prayer,
In the stillness, heartbeats align,
Harmony found everywhere,
In the layers icy divine.

A Song of Solitude's Winter

In the chill, a hush invites,
Snowflakes drift, a gentle flood,
Each one twirls in soft starlights,
A quiet world, where shadows stood.

Branches bow beneath the weight,
Each adorned with winter's lace,
Time moves slow, in stillest state,
Silenced dreams in this cold space.

Footprints fade on powdered white,
Every step a fleeting trace,
In this realm, a pure delight,
Finding solace in still grace.

The evening glows in silver threads,
Moonlight dances on the ground,
Each soft sparkle gently spreads,
Whispers lost in silence found.

Frozen echoes call my name,
In the solitude, I roam,
Embracing all the chill and flame,
A winter's song calls me home.

Still Waters Beneath Ice

Mirrored skies in silent pools,
Reflecting dreams of days gone past,
Underneath, the water cools,
Hidden depths that hold steadfast.

Icebound layers cloaked in white,
Holding secrets, still and deep,
Gentle ripples lost from sight,
In this calmness, silence sleeps.

Nature hums in muted tones,
Crystals spark in twilight's glow,
Underneath, life gently moans,
Waiting for the spring to show.

Echoes linger in the air,
As branches sway in winter's sigh,
Within these waters, moments share,
Time moves slow as swans glide by.

A canvas painted in soft gray,
Capturing every breath and glance,
In still waters, we find our way,
Fate's quiet, yet bold advance.

Emptiness in a Snow-Covered World

Once filled with life, now draped in white,
A barren field, silence reigns,
Echoes hide from morning light,
Nature's grip, a tranquil chain.

Footsteps vanish in fresh snow,
Leaving no mark or trace behind,
In this stillness, currents flow,
Whispers lost in winter's bind.

Trees stand bare, their stories told,
Cloaked in frost, they bow low,
A quiet strength in every fold,
Resilient, despite winter's woe.

The air holds still, each breath a sigh,
As twilight paints the world in gray,
In emptiness, we wonder why,
Yet within, warmth will always stay.

And though the snow may blanket all,
Hope persists amid the white,
A vision waits, through the quiet call,
For spring to break the frozen night.

Quietude in the Morning Frost

A whispering chill greets the dawn,
Blankets of frost on the lawn.
Birds offer songs, soft and slight,
Nature awakens in gentle light.

Trees stand silent, their branches bare,
Crystals glisten, a breath of air.
Footsteps muffled on winter's ground,
In quietude, peace is found.

The sky blushes with hues of gold,
Stories of night will soon unfold.
With every breath, the world stands still,
A tranquil heart, a bending will.

Clouds drift softly, like dreams unchained,
Every moment, beautifully framed.
Time moves gently, like a soft sigh,
In morning's grace, we learn to fly.

Awake, awake! Now feel the frost,
In moments cherished, never lost.
The day awaits, embrace the light,
In quietude, all feels right.

The Stillness That Holds Us

In the hush of twilight's kiss,
We find ourselves in fleeting bliss.
Gentle shadows, softly cast,
Moments linger, forever last.

Silent whispers through the trees,
Carried gently by the breeze.
In the stillness, hearts align,
Time stands still, like aged wine.

Stars awaken in a velvet sky,
As night unfolds, we learn to fly.
The world a canvas, pure and vast,
Painted dreams, unbound, unmasked.

Each heartbeat a quiet song,
In stillness, we find we belong.
Softly, softly, the night unfurls,
A treasure chest of silver pearls.

In the echoes of the night,
Bring your dreams into the light.
Let the stillness wrap you tight,
In this embrace, all feels right.

Secrets Cradled in Winter's Heart

Beneath the snow, a whisper grows,
In silent depths, the secret flows.
Winter cradles what lies beneath,
Hope and dreams wrapped in a sheath.

Icicles guard the truths untold,
Stories of warmth in the bitter cold.
Through the stillness, we hold the key,
To treasures buried, waiting to see.

The moonlight dances on frosty ground,
Echoes of laughter, soft and profound.
In the chill, a warmth ignites,
Through the shadows, life recites.

Years in waiting, a moment's gaze,
In winter's heart, the hidden stays.
Flames flicker in the dark of night,
Cradled secrets, painted bright.

Let the silence be your guide,
In winter's heart, let love abide.
For all the secrets that lie in wait,
In whispered dreams, we seal our fate.

Emptiness in Snow-Draped Dreams

A blanket white covers the land,
In quietude, we take a stand.
Snowflakes fall like whispered sighs,
Draping dreams under winter's eyes.

In the stillness, shadows play,
Echoes of night, fading away.
The world so vast, yet so confined,
In snow-draped dreams, our hearts unwind.

Footsteps vanish in the frost,
All that we've known feels like lost.
Yet in the silence, hope remains,
A tapestry woven with joy and pains.

Close your eyes, let stillness grow,
In every flake, a story flows.
The emptiness sings, a gentle tune,
Under the watchful eye of the moon.

Embrace the peace that fills the night,
In snow-draped dreams, we find our light.
Amidst the cold, a warmth shall gleam,
In emptiness, we forge our dream.

Shadows of Winter's Breath

Whispers of snow on the ground,
Shadows dance, a hush all around.
Branches heavy with icy lace,
Nature rests in a tranquil embrace.

Moonlight glimmers on the frozen stream,
Stars twinkle softly, a silver dream.
Each breath visible, a fleeting sigh,
In winter's grasp, time passes by.

Frost clings to the edges of night,
Silent secrets in the pale twilight.
Echoes of warmth in the heart's wish,
Yet cold is the kiss of the winter's brush.

Footprints left in a snowy glow,
Memories linger in soft and slow.
A world transformed in quiet repose,
Where stillness reigns and the chill wind blows.

Veils of silence enshroud the trees,
Breath of the season whispers through leaves.
In the dusk, shadows gently creep,
As winter's night sings us to sleep.

Stillness Wrapped in White

Blankets of snow on the ground,
In stillness, a quiet peace found.
Nature holds its breath, serene,
A magical hush, pure and clean.

Frosty branches shimmer bright,
Under the calm of the silver light.
Gentle whispers in the air,
A moment of magic, tender and rare.

Soft footsteps crunch on the way,
Chasing the dreams of a winter's day.
The world feels hushed, slow, and wide,
As if wrapped in a cozy tide.

Under a quilt of glistening frost,
Finding joy in what was once lost.
Love woven into each white flake,
In stillness, our weary hearts awake.

The evening fades to a muted hue,
As night whispers secrets to stars anew.
In the quiet, a tranquil light,
Stillness wrapped in snow, pure and bright.

Frosted Dreams at Dawn

Awake with the blush of a winter dawn,
Frosted dreams greet the day, reborn.
Soft light spills on fields of white,
Nature awakes, a beautiful sight.

Glistening crystals on every branch,
In a gentle breeze, branches dance.
Each breath releases a cloud of mist,
Morning beckons with a tender list.

Colors emerge as the sun ascends,
Golden rays the silence mends.
A canvas painted with hues of gold,
Whispers of warmth begin to unfold.

Birds take flight in a choreographed line,
Singing sweet notes that intertwine.
In this moment, all feels so right,
Frosted dreams fade, welcoming light.

Nature wakes from a slumber deep,
Inviting us forth from our sleep.
With hearts aglow and spirits free,
Frosted dreams at dawn, a symphony.

Lament of the Winter Night

Veil of shadows drapes the land,
Winter whispers, cold and grand.
Silence reigns in the darkened sky,
A distant moon begins to cry.

The chill wraps tight, a heavy cloak,
In the night, ancient tales are spoke.
Echoes of laughter in memories stay,
Fading like the light of day.

Winds carry stories through icy trees,
Mournful melodies in the chill breeze.
Stars glimmer like tears in the night,
Each one a wish for warmth and light.

Shadows creep with a ghostly grace,
Loneliness wears a familiar face.
Yet amidst the sorrow, hope ignites,
A flicker of warmth in the coldest nights.

Though winter's heart may seem like stone,
In its embrace, we're never alone.
For in the dark, we find our sight,
In the lament of the winter night.

Milton Keynes UK
Ingram Content Group UK Ltd.
UKHW010231111224
452348UK00011B/677